PAMPHLETS ON AMERICAN WRITERS · NUMBER 47

UNIVERSITY OF MINNESOTA

Hart Crane

BY MONROE K. SPEARS

UNIVERSITY OF MINNESOTA PRESS · MINNEAPOLIS

Printed in the United States of America at
the North Central Publishing Company, St. Paul

Library of Congress Catalog Card Number: 65-63411

Distributed to high schools in the United States by Webster Division
McGraw-Hill Book Company
St. Louis   New York   San Francisco   Dallas

PUBLISHED IN GREAT BRITAIN, INDIA, AND PAKISTAN BY THE OXFORD UNIVERSITY
PRESS, LONDON, BOMBAY, AND KARACHI, AND IN CANADA BY THE COPP
CLARK PUBLISHING CO. LIMITED, TORONTO

HART CRANE

MONROE K. SPEARS, Libbie Shearn Moody Professor of English at Rice University, was editor of the *Sewanee Review* from 1952 to 1961. He is the author of *The Poetry of W. H. Auden: The Disenchanted Island.*

⌃Hart Crane

I‌ₙ "Words for Hart Crane" Robert Lowell called Crane "*Catullus redivivus*" and "the Shelley of my age"; in a recent *Paris Review* interview he said: "I think Crane is the great poet of that generation . . . Not only is it the tremendous power there, but he somehow got New York City: he was at the center of things in the way that no other poet was. All the chaos of his life missed getting sidetracked the way other poets' did, and he was less limited than any other poet of his generation. There was a fulness of experience . . ." As the major poet of a later generation, Lowell speaks with authority, and he expresses an opinion that seems to be increasingly prevalent.

In life and in poetry, Crane was intense, extreme, and uncompromising; he is as effective a flutterer of dovecotes as Catullus or Blake or Rimbaud. He challenges the imagination and compels judgment; no tepid response either to him or to what he stands for is possible. He was unquestionably a man of principle, whatever the merit of his principles. (His severest critic called him "a saint of the wrong religion.") Precisely what was wrong with these principles, aesthetic and religious, was defined early and very fully by several of our most brilliant critics. This was a necessary task, for certainly Crane was a dangerous model and an example variously instructive. Thirty-odd years after his death, however, he has been so disinfected by the passage of time that he is hardly likely to spread any contagions, and it seems more profitable now to focus attention on his achievement than on the nature and significance of his failure. Allen Tate, the finest of the critics who defined Crane's errors, recognized this in adding to his essay "Hart Crane" an "Encomium Twenty Years Later" celebrating Crane as "a great lyric poet" and "our twentieth-century poet as hero."

Crane has been the hero of many cults, on grounds often both dubious and inconsistent. Homosexuals naturally canonized him and made him their patron, as St. Hart the Homintern Martyr (to adapt the title W. H. Auden once gave to Wilde). But Allen Tate, his close friend, calls him "an extreme example of the *unwilling* homosexual" and observes that he was never alienated in the sense of rejecting the full human condition, any more than his poetry rejects the central tradition of the past. Patriots and optimists have sometimes hailed him as the Pindar of machinery, the modern Whitman who celebrates America and proves that our civilization is no Waste Land but a triumphant Bridge. Crane did harbor such aspirations, intermittently, but he was not taken in by them. Social critics from Marxist to Beat have made Crane's "crack-up," like that of F. Scott Fitzgerald, a type of the fate of the writer in modern America. Crane does indeed exhibit all the pressures of our civilization in their most extreme form, though he also furnishes an almost embarrassingly obvious case history for the psychological critic. Finally, Crane has been adulated by the followers of all kinds of poetic unreason; much fake poetry has been perpetrated in his name, and increasingly of late he has been used as a stalking-horse by the Neo-Romantics. It is true that Crane expounded and sometimes practiced a kind of irrationalism or mysticism, as we shall see; but it is also true that he was a meticulous craftsman, seeking not to break with but to follow the central tradition in poetry, and he strove to eliminate obscurity.

Crane's poetry has, then, provided the text for many sermons and the ground for many controversies. The essential fact is, however, that it is still alive as poetry, that it still speaks powerfully both to readers encountering it for the first time and to those who go back to it. Its influence on Allen Tate, Robert Lowell, Dylan Thom-

6

as, and many lesser figures is plain. Now, more than thirty years after his suicide, we can say that his work survives all the contemporary disputes and passions, and that in spite of its small bulk and its obvious limitations and defects, it will remain among the permanent treasures of American poetry in the twentieth century.

Because Crane's life was spectacular and portentous, it tends to distract attention from his poetry. The biographical approach to the poetry is misleading; it gives chief prominence to Crane's personal disintegration and his unsuccessful attempt to create a myth. But these are not the central issues in his work, which, like all true poetry, has a life of its own apart from the poet. I shall therefore confine myself to a short biographical summary before considering the poetry.

Harold Hart Crane was born in Ohio, into the midwestern small-town cultural milieu satirized by Sinclair Lewis and so many others. He was an only child and the product of a broken home; his childhood was dominated by the tension between his parents, who first separated in 1909, when Hart was ten, sending him to live with his maternal grandmother. His father, a hard-headed businessman highly successful in the manufacture of candy and in other enterprises, was remote from his son and showed him small understanding or sympathy. The mother enveloped and dominated him, turning him bitterly against the father and dragging him through all their quarrels (he said later that his childhood had been a "bloody battleground" for his parents' sex lives). This classic Oedipal situation was no doubt the basis of his homosexuality and his other psychological peculiarities. After quarrels, separations, and temporary reconciliations spanning Hart's childhood and early adolescence, the parents were finally divorced, and both later remarried. Hart had, of course, taken his mother's side throughout the quarrels — he had traveled with her through the West and to the Isle of

7

Pines, south of Cuba — and after the divorce he symbolically truncated his name, using the maternal surname "Hart" as his first name and thus rejecting the father who had rejected him. In 1916, at the age of seventeen, he abandoned high school and went alone to New York to live. In this year he had published his first poem and prose piece (he had begun to write three years before), and he now committed himself irrevocably to poetry as a vocation.

Crane emerged from this background emotionally crippled, morbidly overstimulated, rootless, and unable ever to adjust to a "normal" pattern of living. Like most Americans, he cherished the notion of making quick money by writing a movie scenario or a popular story or novel; but aside from brief periods working in bookstores, in his father's factories and candy stores, and as a salesman, his closest approaches to success in earning a living were as an advertising copy writer — a profession chiefly dedicated to the debasement of language and the deception of the public. New York, citadel and symbol of the pressures toward rootlessness and alienation, was inevitably the place he would live most of the time, and partly in the underground world of the homosexual.

When Crane went to New York in 1916, one of the books he took with him was Mary Baker Eddy's *Science and Health with Key to the Scriptures*. Both his mother and her mother were fervent advocates of Christian Science, and although Hart did not remain a believer in it as a religion for long, he remained convinced of its psychological efficacy. He wrote in 1919: "What it says in regard to mental and nervous ailments is absolutely true. It is only the total denial of the animal and organic world which I cannot swallow." His training in this faith, with the influence and example of the two people to whom he was closest, had a lasting effect on him. Born out of the union of American transcendentalism and American hypochondria, Christian Science holds that states of consciousness are the only reality, that matter is unreal, that all causation is mental and apparent evil the result of erring belief. Crane's predisposition to optimism and irrationalism and his later pseudo-mystical strivings for the "higher consciousness" undoubtedly owe much to this early background.

A similar and perhaps even more powerful influence in the formation of his aesthetic and religious attitudes was his early study of Plato. According to Philip Horton, Crane's earliest biographer, he underscored doubly with red ink the passages on the necessity of madness in a true poet, and the Platonic concept of a progression upward from earthly beauties in a search for absolute beauty became fundamental to his thought. Nietzsche, about whom Crane wrote an article as early as 1918, also played an important part in his development. Nietzsche's anti-philistinism, his exaltation of the artist, and his celebration of Dionysian joy appealed strongly to Crane and merged with other powerful currents. One such was the *Tertium Organum* (first published in the United States in 1920) of P. D. Ouspensky, a rhapsodic and pseudo-mystical work from which Crane took the phrase "higher consciousness," and which advocated the Dionysian type of mystical experience and the artist as guide to spiritual truth. Other currents in the mystical and pantheistic stream were the Bengali poet Rabindranath Tagore, whom Crane met in Cleveland in 1916, and such visionary and antirational poets as Blake, who exerted a powerful and continuing influence on Crane, and Rimbaud, whose disciple and heir Crane early came to consider himself.

Counterbalancing these powerful tendencies toward irrationalism, mysticism, and occultism was Crane's relation to his American literary heritage. When he was fifteen he spent several weeks at the establishment of Elbert Hubbard, a highly successful purveyor of culture and homely philosophy to the American public; as one of Crane's biographers, Brom Weber, puts it, he "capitalized upon the contradictory and confused American temper at the turn of the century by clothing materialism with an atmosphere of romance and culture." But, if he contributed to Crane's decision to go into advertising and his belief that he could somehow make money out of literature, he also helped to acquaint Crane with the classic American poets. Crane recognized early, at a time when it was by no means the truism it is now, that the great American writers were Whitman, Melville, Dickinson, and James, with Poe as progenitor and type. (He seems not to have been aware of Hawthorne.) Through Mrs. William Vaughn Moody, who befriended him, he became acquainted with some of the new writers and the "little magazines" that were their chief media of publication; and he also knew the older generation of writers such as Sherwood Anderson, Lindsay, Masters, and Sandburg.

Though Crane was from the beginning intensely aware of the new movements and the emerging writers, and though Pound and Eliot were soon to become his chief mentors, it is curious and interesting that the dominant influences on his early poetry (roughly 1916–20) were Swinburne, the early Yeats, and especially Wilde, Dowson, and the other "Decadents." *Bruno's Weekly* and *Bruno's Bohemia* frequently reprinted the works of Dowson and Wilde and praised Wilde's life and writings; Crane's first poem, called "C 33" (Wilde's designation in Reading Gaol), appeared in the former in 1916 and his "Carmen de Boheme" in the latter two years later; both are, as the titles suggest, *fin de siècle* in spirit and conventional in form. Crane's first published prose, a letter to *The Pagan* (1916), reveals the way ninetyish aestheticism and the "new" coexisted harmoniously in the literary awareness of the time. He said, "I am interested in your magazine as a new and distinctive chord in the present American Renaissance of literature and art. Let me praise your September cover; it has some suggestion of the exoticism and richness of Wilde's poems." New York in the winter of 1916–17 was especially exciting, not only because of the war, but because the literary "American Renaissance" of which Crane spoke was at its height. Since the founding of *Poetry* by Harriet Monroe in 1912 numerous "little magazines" had been established and many anthologies, as well as volumes by individual poets, had appeared. There had been much agitation about Imagism, with Amy Lowell taking over the movement from Ezra Pound. In 1917 Pound transferred his allegiance from *Poetry* to the *Little Review*, which had just moved from Chicago to New York; thenceforth the *Little Review* followed his cosmopolitan aim of bringing together the best English writers (Eliot, Joyce, Lewis, Pound) and French (de Gourmont, Rimbaud, Laforgue, Corbière) with the best of the Americans — a program cultivated by *The Dial* also after 1920. Other magazines, notably *The Seven Arts*, had a more nationalistic emphasis.

These magazines, and numerous others with such names as *The Egoist, Blast, The Modern School, The Modernist*, were the main agents of Crane's self-education. His chief teachers in this equivalent of higher education (and these were precisely the years during which he would have been attending a college or university, in the normal course of affairs) were Pound and Eliot, with Pound first dominating (as early as 1917) and then, a year or two later, Eliot most decisively. Both as critics and as poets, they form his taste, stimulate and provoke him, and teach him the craft of poetry. It is through them that he discovers the Elizabethans and Metaphysicals (special enthusiasms being Donne, Marlowe, and Webster), Dante (whom he did not, however, study intensively until 1930), and most overwhelmingly the French poets from Baudelaire on.

By 1921, Crane had achieved full poetic maturity, finding his own voice, style, and themes; and in the same year he broke decisively with his father. From his first departure for New York in 1916 until this time, he had felt the "curse of sundered parentage" with particular virulence. He had returned to Cleveland and had lived in Akron and Washington, D.C., for varying periods in response to pleas from his mother or offers of work in various capacities (all humble—clerk, salesman, supervisor) in his father's candy business. The year 1921 did not mark the achievement of any sort of stability, emotional or economic, but it may be said to signal the end of the process of education and definition of himself as poet and as person.

The external events of the rest of his life require little space to describe. In the single decade remaining to him, he tried with small success to find a satisfactory means of support in advertising or other hackwork. The increasing disorder of his personal life, dominated by alcoholism and homosexuality, made the various forms of temporary patronage he finally received of little use to him. The chief of these were a grant from the banker Otto Kahn in 1925 and a Guggenheim fellowship in 1931, though he also served briefly as traveling secretary to a wealthy stockbroker and enjoyed the extended hospitality of Harry and Caresse Crosby in Paris. His first volume, *White Buildings*, was published (after many delays and difficulties) in 1926. In the same year he made another stay on the Isle of Pines, writing there many of the poems collected as *Key West: An Island Sheaf* and published posthumously, and much of *The Bridge*. Late in 1928 he sailed for Europe, spending the first half of 1929 mostly in Paris, where he found society all too congenial to his vices. The Crosbys did, however, provide him with the stimulus to finish *The Bridge* — which Crane had begun in 1923 and worked on at intervals since — by undertaking to print it at their Black Sun Press in Paris; it was published both there and in New York in 1930. In 1931 he went to Mexico on his Guggenheim fellowship, projecting an epic on the conquest of Mexico; but in spite of devoted efforts by several people to help him — Hans Zinsser, the famous bacteriologist; Katherine Anne Porter, his neighbor in Mexico; and

Peggy Baird, former wife of Malcolm Cowley, with whom he lived for a time in a last approach to heterosexual love — he was able to do little writing. Quarrelsome, drunk much of the time, alternating between manic exhilaration and suicidal depression, he had little control of himself and was frequently on, and sometimes across, the border of insanity. He did produce one last poem as good as anything he ever wrote, "The Broken Tower," in February–March 1932. A month later he leaped from the stern of the ship taking him from Mexico to the United States, acting out the symbolism of many of his poems by drowning in the Caribbean. A final symbolic touch was added to the story when his mother died in 1947 and her ashes were scattered, according to her directions, from Brooklyn Bridge.

Crane's talent was astonishing indeed to survive the extreme disorder of his life and all the other forces inimical to it and enable him in spite of everything to produce poetry of lasting value. But Crane was by no means passive, a mere vessel; his attitude toward his poetry was much more conservative and shrewd and disciplined than the sensational outlines of his life would suggest. His constant effort was to educate himself poetically, to discipline his gifts, to establish a valid relation to tradition. He was rarely taken in by fads or extremists, and his critical comments show great penetration. His letters, collected in 1952, seem to me the most impressive since Keats's, and fully worthy of comparison to them; they are profoundly moving human documents, colorful, penetrating, often humorous, and rich in moral insight (unexpected as this quality might seem). The book has long been out of print, but its quality will, I am sure, eventually come to be recognized. The letters reveal much about the nature of our civilization in that crucial period 1916–32, and the symptomatic aspect of Crane's career; they also have the special human interest and pathos of portraying the artist who dies young and as victim. (He wrote in 1922, "I shall do my best work later on when I am about 35 or 40.")

The challenge of Crane's poetry called forth from several of our best critics essays that remain classics. Such are Allen Tate's crucial pieces, R. P. Blackmur's explorations of how Crane's language works, and Yvor Winters' definitions of how Crane was misled by the "American religion" of Whitman and Emerson. Full-length studies of Crane's poetry and his life have likewise been of high caliber. Philip Horton's biography of 1937 is exceptionally readable without sacrifice of thoroughness and accuracy. Brom Weber's study, a decade later, presented much further information; Weber also skillfully edited Crane's letters. L. S. Dembo's study (1960) of *The Bridge* is an impressive Neo-Romantic interpretation. The latest books (both 1963) by Samuel Hazo and Vincent Quinn are useful brief introductions.

To turn now to specific discussion of the poetry. Of the 28 poems in *White Buildings*, all but two were written in 1920–25, and most of them in the latter part of that period. (The two Crane chose to preserve from the large number he had produced before 1920 were "North Labrador" and "In Shadow.") They are all mature work, and an approach in terms of development and chronology is not very revealing. Perhaps the best way is to begin with some poems about the nature of poetry and the poet.

"Chaplinesque" is an early and relatively simple presentation of one aspect of the situation of the poet.

> We make our meek adjustments,
> Contented with such random consolations
> As the wind deposits
> In slithered and too ample pockets.
>
> For we can still love the world, who find
> A famished kitten on the step, and know
> Recesses for it from the fury of the street,
> Or warm torn elbow coverts.

It was inspired by Chaplin's *The Kid*, and Crane explained his intentions in several letters: "I am moved to put Chaplin with the poets [of today]; hence the 'we.' . . . Poetry, the human feelings, 'the kitten,' is so crowded out of the humdrum, rushing, mechanical scramble of today that the man who would preserve them must duck and camouflage for dear life to keep them or keep himself from annihilation. . . . I feel that I have captured the arrested climaxes and evasive victories of his gestures in words, somehow . . . I have made that 'infinitely gentle, infinitely suffering thing' of Eliot's into the symbol of the kitten."

The Romantic irony of the clown-poet figure and the tone and language of this poem suggest the French Symbolists, whom Crane had been studying; he had recently translated three poems by Laforgue. But the poem also illustrates a more distinctive and lasting influence: that of the graphic arts. Fundamental to Crane's aesthetic was the similarity between poetry and painting (and such related graphic arts as photography). Painting was, from early adolescence, almost as important to him as poetry, and he surrounded himself with prints as well as books. When he went to New York in 1916, Carl Schmitt, a young painter, went over Crane's work, giving him the benefit of the painter's sensitive response to rhythm and movement. They agreed, according to Horton, that Crane ". . . should compose a certain number of poems a week simply as technical exercises with the purpose of breaking down formal patterns. These he would bring to his critic as he wrote them, and the two would read them over together, Schmitt illustrating with pencil on paper the rising and falling of cadences, the dramatic effect of caesural breaks, and the general movement of the poem as a whole. . . . Surprisingly enough, this conscious experimentation with verse forms did not lead him, as it might well have done during those flourishing days of *vers libre*, to abandon meter and rhyme." Both Schmitt and Crane also composed nonsense verses in which meaning played no part; the main purpose was to exploit the sounds of words and letters as if they were musical notes.

After his return to Cleveland, Crane became friendly with a group of painters who further stimulated his interest in the art and taught him much about it. His closest friend among them was William Sommers, whom he celebrated in "Sunday Morning Apples"; in this poem the "Beloved apples of seasonable madness" are transfigured by art in a Dionysiac metamorphosis, poised "full and ready for explosion." Specific paintings by El Greco and Joseph Stella provided part of the inspiration for *The Bridge*, and the analogy with painting seemed to be constantly in Crane's mind. As Horton puts it, his attitude toward his poems "was primarily plastic. . . . Crane intended these poems not as descriptions of experience that could be *read about*, but as immediate experiences that the reader could *have* . . ."

In replying to a friend's request for an explanation of "Black Tambourine," Crane said, "The value of the poem is only, to me, in what a painter would call its 'tactile' quality, — an entirely aesthetic feature. A propagandist for either side of the Negro question could find anything he wanted to in it. My only declaration in it is that I find the Negro (in the popular mind) sentimentally or brutally 'placed' in this midkingdom, etc." This remark is especially interesting because Crane is denying any intentional concern with a social and moral value that is certainly in the poem. Crane is, of course, right when he says that it is a "bundle of insinuations, suggestions," remote from propaganda; but its imaginative apprehension of the Negro's plight is not a purely aesthetic phenomenon:

> The interests of a black man in a cellar
> Mark tardy judgment on the world's closed door.
> Gnats toss in the shadow of a bottle,
> And a roach spans a crevice in the floor.

Æsop, driven to pondering, found
Heaven with the tortoise and the hare . . .

In the light of later events, readers now can hardly avoid calling the poem prophetic, though its prophecy is not the vision of a seer but the best kind of social consciousness and moral perceptiveness. (It was written in 1921.) The Negro in the cellar (driven underground, pushed out of sight) regards the "world's closed door." His situation keeps him dirty and drives him to drink (at least this is one interpretation of the bottle and the roach). The second stanza considers Aesop, who perhaps would not have pondered had he not been a slave, and notes that he counseled patience in his fable of the tortoise and the hare; he "found Heaven" with them in the sense that he achieved literary immortality, but the "Fox brush and sow ear" on his grave suggest ironically that his solution was not complete. Aesop is appropriate here also because so many of the Uncle Remus stories derive from him, and the images of the ancient and the modern slaves fuse: both wise, both counseling resignation and patience ("Uncle Toms" in contemporary language), and both dead — i.e., the situation has changed. The "mingling incantations" suggests both the remains of primitive superstition and the singing of Negroes. The last stanza puts explicitly the dilemma of the Negro, wandering forlorn between his recent past in America, symbolized by the tambourine of the minstrel show, when he could be regarded merely as a clown, a stock figure of fun, and his savage and primitive origins in Africa, symbolized by the "carcass quick with flies." But the day of the minstrel show is past; the tambourine is stuck on the wall, and the Negro has been closed up in the cellar. The poem has a poise and taut restraint that are remarkable, and an intensity of perception not inferior to the more obviously emotional later poems.

"Praise for an Urn" is an elegy for Ernest Nelson, at whose

funeral in December 1921 Crane, with Sommers, had been a pall-bearer. Nelson was a Norwegian who had come to the United States at fifteen, gone to art school and done some good paintings and written some good poems, but then been forced to go into lithography to make a living. Crane called him "One of the best-read people I ever met, wonderful kindliness and tolerance and a true Nietzschean. He was one of many broken against the stupidity of American life . . ." The funeral, Crane said, was "tremendous, especially the finale at the crematorium . . . That funeral was one of the few beautiful things that have happened to me in Cleveland." I have quoted these remarks from Crane's letters because they reveal the feelings that went into the poem and contrast with its poise and restraint; they also clarify some of its allusions.

> It was a kind and northern face
> That mingled in such exile guise
> The everlasting eyes of Pierrot
> And, of Gargantua, the laughter. . . .

In this first stanza, "exile" is richly ambiguous: the Mediterranean qualities of Pierrot and Gargantua lived, in exile, in Nelson's "northern" face, and Pierrot, the pathetic clown, and Gargantua, who laughed at the serious world, counterbalance each other nicely. Further, Nelson was himself in exile both from his original Norwegian home and from the world of art, as he worked in his Cleveland lithography factory. His thoughts (in the second stanza) passed on to Crane were "inheritances" — tradition in the literal sense — but in a world where traditions are increasingly precarious, "Delicate riders of the storm," and Crane hopes to pass them on in turn. The third stanza describes shared experiences in which they discussed such traditions (and perhaps more personal kinds of immortality also); but the clock of the fourth contradicts this, with its insistent comment reminding of death.

Survival even in memory is dubious in the penultimate stanza, and the last bids an ironic and resigned farewell to the friend's ashes and to the elegy ("these well-meant idioms"); both will be scattered and lost in the smoky spring of the typical modern suburbs.

These two poems in quatrains exhibit a moral and aesthetic poise, as well as a moral penetration and awareness, rare in Crane's later work. The major poems of the next few years follow a new line and method of composition. A letter to his good friend Gorham Munson points the direction. He had had a mystical experience in a dentist's chair — an anesthetic revelation: ". . . under the influence of aether and *amnesia* my mind spiraled to a kind of seventh heaven of consciousness and egoistic dance among the seven spheres — and something like an objective voice kept saying to me — 'You have the higher consciousness — you have the higher consciousness. This is something that very few have. This is what is called genius' . . . A happiness, ecstatic such as I have known only twice in 'inspirations' came over me. I felt the two worlds. And at once. . . . O Gorham, I have known moments in eternity."

The essence of Crane's later poetic may be found in "The Wine Menagerie." The title indicates very precisely the whole theme of the poem. "Menagerie" suggests both a collection of wild animals and, etymologically, a household; hence it evokes immediately the central image of the contents of the mind as wild animals. (Yeats's "Circus Animals' Desertion" uses a very similar metaphor.) "Wine" suggests that the menagerie exists (or, perhaps, that the animals become wild) only through the stimulus and release of alcohol. When "wine redeems the sight," then a "leopard ranging always in the brow / Asserts a vision in the slumbering gaze." The lying reality of everyday ("glozening decanters that reflect the street" as the poet sits in a bar) is transcended; the poet sees "New thresholds, new anatomies! Wine talons / Build freedom up about me . . ." But the whole experience is viewed with romantic irony: the wild animals are dangerous to the poet, and the world not really transcended: "Ruddy, the tooth implicit of the world / Has followed you." The poet is betrayed, his head separated from his body like those of Holofernes and John the Baptist; and he is as ineffectual as the puppet Petrushka's valentine. This is, of course, the notion of the poet as visionary and seer, capable of a higher consciousness, a divine madness, which Crane took primarily from Blake and Rimbaud (who provide the epigraphs for two of his three volumes) and ultimately from Plato and Nietzsche. Crane, notoriously, often strove to achieve this condition through the stimulus both of alcohol and of a phonograph playing loudly and repetitiously.

In "General Aims and Theories," he described his poetic theory at some length. The core of this essay is Crane's insistence that he is not an impressionist, but an "absolutist." The impressionist, he says, "is interesting as far as he goes — but his goal has been reached when he has succeeded in projecting certain selected factual details into his reader's consciousness. He is really not interested in the *causes* (metaphysical) of his materials, their emotional derivations or their utmost spiritual consequences. A kind of retinal registration is enough, along with a certain psychological stimulation. And this is also true of your realist . . . and to a certain extent of the classicist . . . Blake meant these differences when he wrote:

> We are led to believe in a lie
> When we see *with* not *through* the eye."

The absolutist, however — and the predecessors Crane cites are Donne, Blake, Baudelaire, and Rimbaud — hopes to "go *through* the combined materials of the poem, using our 'real' world somewhat as a spring-board, and to give the poem *as a whole* an orbit or predetermined direction of its own." Such a poem aims at freedom from the personalities of both poet and reader, and is "at least a stab at a truth"; hence it may be called "absolute." Crane then suggests the kind of truth such poetry attempts to embody: "Its evocation will not be toward decoration or amusement, but rather toward a state of consciousness, an 'innocence' (Blake) or absolute beauty. In this condition there may be discoverable under new forms certain spiritual illuminations, shining with a morality essentialized from experience directly, and not from previous precepts or preconceptions. It is as though a poem gave the reader as he left it a single, new *word*, never before spoken and impossible to actually enunciate, but self-evident as an active principle in the reader's consciousness henceforward." As to technique, Crane says that the "terms of expression" employed are often selected less for their logical or literal than for their associational meanings: "Via this and their metaphorical inter-relationships, the entire construction of the poem is raised on the organic principle of a 'logic of metaphor,' which antedates our so-called pure logic, and which is the genetic basis of all speech, hence consciousness and thought-extension."

He then goes on to explain and defend the difficulty of his poems in terms of these principles, speaking of the "implicit emotional dynamics of the materials used" and the "organic impact of the imagination" of the poem; the poet's business, he says, is the "conquest of consciousness." In a letter to Harriet Monroe, he put it more plainly: "as a poet I may very possibly be more interested in the so-called illogical impingements of the connotations of words on the consciousness (and their combinations and interplay in metaphor on this basis) than I am interested in the preservation of their logically rigid significations at the cost of limiting my subject matter and perceptions involved in the poem." And in the essay "Modern Poetry," he casts further light on his notion of poetic truth: "poetic prophecy in the case of the seer has nothing to do with factual prediction or with futurity. It is a peculiar type of perception, capable of apprehending some absolute and timeless concept of the imagination with astounding clarity and conviction."

We may now consider some of the poems in *White Buildings* that follow and exemplify this poetic. "Recitative" begins:

> Regard the capture here, O Janus-faced,
> As double as the hands that twist this glass.
> Such eyes at search or rest you cannot see;
> Reciting pain or glee, how can you bear!

It is so very difficult that even Allen Tate had trouble with it, and Crane wrote an apologetic explanation to him: "Imagine the poet, say, on a platform speaking it. The audience is one half of Humanity, Man (in the sense of Blake) and the poet the other. ALSO, the poet sees himself in the audience as in a mirror. ALSO, the audience sees itself, in part, in the poet. Against this paradoxical DUALITY is posed the UNITY . . . in the last verse. In another sense, the poet is *talking to himself* all the way through the poem, and there are, as too often in my poems, other reflexes and symbolisms in the poem, also, which it would be silly to write here . . ." As usual in explaining his own poems, Crane begins here by describing the dramatic situation, and his comments, as always, are convincing and helpful; but they are far from resolving the difficulties of the poem. The situation itself is so ambiguous, with so many alternative interpretations (as Crane indicates), that visualizing it is not much help. The fourth stanza is the source of the title of the volume:

> Look steadily — how the wind feasts and spins
> The brain's disk shivered against lust. Then watch
> While darkness, like an ape's face, falls away,
> And gradually white buildings answer day.

The white buildings, contrasted with darkness and the ape's face, are embodiments of the Ideal, testaments of the Word; they are, specifically, poems of the sort Crane is writing. They are also, of course, New York skyscrapers transfigured by the dawn light. It is worth noting that the redemption takes place although — or perhaps because — the brain is unable to control lust. The next two stanzas describe the magnificence and isolation of the skyscrapers, and urge: "leave the tower" for the bridge — abandon isolation for unity. The final stanza evokes unity in the image of "All hours clapped dense into a single stride" in the sound of "alternating bells." Crane called the poem "a confession," and certainly the contrast between the violent dualisms and the final vision of unity is characteristic; the images of the Bridge and the Tower also anticipate strikingly the use Crane was to make of them in later poems.

"Passage" is another difficult and visionary poem. Biographically, it probably derives from the feeling of refreshment Crane experienced in spending the summer of 1925 in the country. This is, however, very little help. The poem is about the experience of vision, of "higher consciousness," which is for Crane synonymous with the writing of poetry; it is in this respect like "The Wine Menagerie," though the perspective here is autobiographical, through time and distance, rather than a close-up as there of the physiological aids and the experience itself. The title suggests a voyage, as often in Crane, and perhaps also the anthropologist's *rite de passage*, a farewell to childhood. The first four stanzas describe the experience of the visionary voyage, promising "an improved infancy" — i.e., a rebirth, a return to innocence. Memory, described scornfully in the second stanza, is left behind. The feeling is of heightened life, of unity with nature, and the voyage almost reaches its goal (the valleys are in sight); but the wind dies, the vision fails, through time and smoke (the evil in man's heart? "chimney-sooted heart of man"), as so often ("a too well-known

23

biography"). The speaker returns to the ravine where he left Memory, and finds a thief beneath the "opening laurel," holding the poet's book. (The laurel is opening because the poet is beginning to gain some reputation; the thief is presumably Memory, or perhaps the Intellect—those faculties, at any rate, that the poet as visionary has abandoned.) After a brief dialogue, Memory closes the book (perhaps in sign of reconciliation), and there is a further visionary experience: History (the sand from the Ptolemies) and Time (the serpent) bring consciousness of past and future (unpaced beaches), and there are further incommunicable revelations ("What fountains . . . speeches?") which overstrain Memory. One meaning (and here, as in much of the preceding, I follow Dembo) would seem to be that Memory is accepted as part of the visionary experience, necessary to it in its mature form, as opposed to the simpler childish form described in the first four stanzas. The poem is evocative of Rimbaud, though very much Crane's own; it has a peculiar intensity, a haunting quality that is remarkable.

"Paraphrase" describes a different kind of vision. It had its inception, according to Horton, in Crane's experience of waking from a drunken sleep into the bright morning light and thinking himself dead. The first two stanzas evoke such an experience: "One rushing from the bed at night" finds, more or less reassuringly, the "record wedged in his soul" of the regular and dependable alternations of life in its various cycles of light and dark, sleeping and waking, expansion and contraction, and the like. The "steady winking beat between / Systole, diastole" suggests such devices as the cardiograph which attest and observe the regularity of the life processes; the tone is clinical. The following phrase, "spokes-of-a-wheel," however, suggests the hysterical and terrifying quality of the experience, as these processes seem speeded up in panic until the alternations blur and seem to reverse, like the spokes of a rapidly revolving wheel. The second stanza represents the sleeper's nightmarish experience with ironic detachment: to the sleeper death has seemed a physical force or object trying to get in between the sheets and immobilize his fingers and toes ("integers of life" suggests also the integrity and unity of body and soul that constitutes life). The last two stanzas evoke that inevitable morning when the experience will be real and not illusory, when the sleeper will really (in the language of folk humor) wake up to find himself dead. However "desperate" the light, however systematically morning floods the pillow, until it is like an "antarctic blaze" of whiteness, it "shall not rouse" the sleeper, whose head will only post "a white paraphrase" among the "bruised roses" of the wallpaper. The word "paraphrase" suggests, together with the "record" of the first stanza, an analogy between the inadequacy as descriptions of natural processes of records such as the cardiogram and the inadequacy of the dead body as equivalent of the living man who was an "integer," a unity. In the simplest terms, the dead body is a paraphrase (with the connotations both of "translation" and of "explanation") and a poor one, of the living man.

Of course I should not insist on any exclusive validity for this reading, though I hope it is convincing enough to demonstrate, at least, that the poem is not centrally obscure. It is difficult, but with a tension and power inseparable from the difficulty. The comparatively regular four-stress lines arranged in quatrains with only an approximation to rhyme in each stanza until the last, when "paraphrase" emerges as a full rhyme to "blaze," produce an effect of climactic intensity.

"Possessions," which follows in *White Buildings*, returns to the visionary theme with its characteristic obscurity. The situation would seem to be that the poet is embarking on a new (homosexual) affair, driven by his lust, and almost sure that this affair will turn out like all the others, but going on nevertheless with his tormented seeking. The first stanza contrasts the rain, which has direction, and the key, which finds its proper lock and turns its bolts, with the poet's "undirected" condition and his phallic "fixed stone of lust" which is no key. The second stanza recites the total of such past experiences. The third places the poet specifically in Greenwich Village, apprehensive beyond words, inspecting his lust, and "turning on smoked forking spires" — the image is apparently of being roasted as on a turnspit over the "city's stubborn lives, desires." The last stanza changes the metaphor to the poet as gored by the horns of lust (as bullfighter or simple victim?); he who "bleeding dies" after such goring achieves nothing but "piteous admissions" to make up a "record of rage and partial appetites." But in spite of all there is the final affirmation:

> The pure possession, the inclusive cloud
> Whose heart is fire shall come, — the white wind raze
> All but bright stones wherein our smiling plays.

The word "possession" has, of course, the double sense of amorous consummation, with the pure one to wash away all the preceding impure (in the sense both of unchaste and of adulterated) experiences, and the supernatural or diabolical sense of being possessed by another spirit and personality; there is perhaps also the third sense of possessions as merely the physical things one owns. The pure possession, when it comes, will be a guiding force like the Biblical pillar of fire by night and pillar of cloud by day, with the myth rationalized to mean that the heart of the cloud must be fire — or, to put it crudely, that passion is the only guide. When the state of possession, of ecstasy (in the etymological sense) is complete (for "partial appetites" are worthless), then the troublesome and archaic stone of lust will be transformed into "bright stones wherein our smiling plays." But one serious difficulty with the poem is that the logical and rhetorical relation of the last three lines to the rest of the poem is not clear. Perhaps the "pure possession" is death — its fiery and destructive force suggests this — and the "bright stones" of the last line are seen only after the purgation of death, as the kind of automatic resurrection or guaranteed paradise suggested in many other poems. But the primary suggestion would seem to be a contrast between those who die through failure to achieve complete appetites, pure possessions, and those who do achieve them and therefore do not die. The poem seems to me, however, far less effective than "Paraphrase," partly because of this central ambiguity.

I have thought it better to present reasonably detailed accounts of those poems in *White Buildings* that seem to me central to Crane's achievement than to attempt to mention all of them, though this has meant omitting, for instance, "Repose of Rivers," Crane's most magical example of incantation and control of sound. Something must be said briefly, however, of "At Melville's Tomb." Crane placed it immediately before the series of "Voyages" at the end of the volume, and it forms a kind of prelude to them, introducing the Voyage symbol which had been implicit in many of the preceding poems. Crane wrote a famous letter (reprinted in Horton's appendix) to Harriet Monroe, editor of *Poetry*, explaining the poem and defending it against her objections; the letter is too long to quote, but may be recommended as containing Crane's detailed explications of some of his most intricate images. The poem seems to me notable, however, as a tribute to Melville and an introduction to "Voyages" rather than as an achievement in its own right.

"Voyages" is, in my judgment, Crane's best long poem. The first section was written in 1921 and an early version of the sixth in 1923, all the rest in 1924–25. Some of the literary inspiration came from the poems of Samuel Greenberg, which Crane had read in manuscript (Greenberg had died in 1916 at the age of twenty-three); but the principal inspiration was Crane's affair with an imaginative and sensitive sailor-lover. As Horton says, "Possibly no other writer but Melville has ever been able to express the mysteries and terrors of the sea with such eloquence and imagination . . ." and this is probably part of the explanation of Eugene O'Neill's enthusiasm for Crane's poetry.

The first section, written much earlier than the others, is much less ambitious. Crane originally called it "The Bottom of the Sea Is Cruel" and, in a letter, "Poster" (saying deprecatingly, "There is nothing more profound in it than a 'stop, look and listen' sign"); the latter title is indicative of its attractive simplicity. The contrast of the children's innocence and gaiety and the mystery, the cruelty and terror, the lightning and thunder of the sea (in the depths beyond the "fresh ruffles" of the surf) is almost Wordsworthian. Its sense of the sea's fatal attraction, which will render the warning to the children futile, foreshadows the theme of the rest of the poem. Compared to the other sections, it is minor art; but it forms an effective introduction to the sequence.

Section II is the most widely anthologized and admired part of the poem; Winters called it "one of the most powerful and one of the most nearly perfect poems of the last two hundred years." Rhetorically, this section would seem to be a counterstatement to the first: the sea is cruel, "And yet" it exempts lovers from its cruelty, regarding them with special favor and sympathy. The sea is a "great wink of eternity" — the wink as sign of complicity and secrets shared only with lovers. (The image also suggests, perhaps, wink as lapse of attention, and hence the sea as escape from time.) Her vast belly bending moonward (and the connotation is not only of the tides but the moon as patron of lovers) is "Laughing the wrapt inflections of our love" — and on one level the image is of the sea as a fat old woman, a bawd or go-between for lovers (like Juliet's nurse), laughing at their raptures while encouraging them and participating in them. This connotation is quali-

fied by the preceding image of the sea as "Samite sheeted and pro-
cessioned" — the Lady of the Lake and other exalted or mysterious ladies in Arthurian legend wore white samite (often with gold
thread), and these qualities of remoteness, legendary and ritualis-
tic and awesome, are attributed to the sea.

The dominant image of the second stanza is of the sea as Judge,
terrible and severe to all but lovers: "The sceptred terror of whose
sessions rends . . . All but the pieties of lovers' hands." The next
stanza explores this partiality of the sea to lovers: as the undersea
bells of the sunken cathedral answer and correspond to the stars
reflected on the surface of the sea, so "Adagios of islands" complete the "dark confessions" spelled by her veins. Crane explained
the former phrase in "General Aims and Theories": ". . . the reference is to the motion of a boat through islands clustered thick-
ly, the rhythm of the motion, etc. And it seems a much more direct
and creative statement than any more logical employment of words
such as 'coasting slowly through the islands,' besides ushering in
a whole world of music." Presumably the meaning is that the
rhythm of the blood in the lover's veins (and "O my Prodigal"
addresses Crane's lover directly for the first time) echoes and corresponds to the sea's rhythm (as the stars and bells have echoed
each other above). The dark confession is, then, that the sea is
like the lover's feelings; her veins are like his veins.

The next stanza draws a kind of conclusion: since the sea (or
love) is in time ("her turning shoulders wind the hours"), the lovers should commit themselves to time and "Hasten, while they
are true," for "sleep, death, desire" (and the equation of all three
is highly significant) are all as much in time, as transient, as "one
floating flower." The magnificent last stanza is a prayer (to vague
and pantheistic deities of sky and sea — clear Seasons and minstrel galleons) that the lovers may be allowed enough time and
committed fully enough to it, and granted enough sense of won-

der ("Bind us in time . . . and awe"), to penetrate the secret—which will mean death. Being bequeathed to an "earthly shore" would mean, presumably, abandoning the life of passion and remaining alive. The grave is a "vortex" which will reveal the sea's depths and secrets and hence answer (provide the only fulfillment of) the "seal's wide spindrift gaze toward paradise." (The last image suggests the equation of sea and death once more: spindrift is windblown spray, hence sea united with air, as the seal is a sea creature which breathes air and has humanoid eyes.) Crane is not asking to live long enough to learn the secret, as some commentators have said, but to remain in the element of the sea—i.e., the passionate life, or love—until he learns the secret through dying.

The third section continues the exploration of the blood relation ("Infinite consanguinity") between the sea and time-bound love and death; in a sense it develops and explains the somewhat cryptic images of the last stanza of the preceding section. The first image is of the relation between sea and sky (the otherworldly, the paradisal) imagined as together supporting the lover's body as "tendered theme." But death is also present in the "reliquary hands" of the sea. The second stanza presents the dramatic climax or resolution: the poet therefore will commit himself, immerse himself in the destructive element (there is no echo of Conrad, but the theme is closely parallel), in the faith that death "Presumes no carnage, but this single change,— . . . The silken skilled transmemberment of song"—a sea-change like that in the *Tempest*, which Crane called the "crown of all the Western world," or like Eliot's "Death by Water," but without any of Eliot's dual possibilities of outcome or supernatural significance; this is a purely secular baptism into passion, with its closest parallel Wagner's "Liebestod." The fusion is complete in the last line, where "love" is both the lover and the sea (the exaltation of poetry and the state of being in love): "Permit me voyage, love, into your hands."

Sections II and III seem to me the best parts of the poem. The chief point I shall hope to establish concerning the remaining parts is that the poem constitutes a genuine sequence and unity. In IV, the lovers are separated and the sea (which literally separates them) is imagined as the element that unites them (for love is a voyage upon this element, this passionate state of being) and conveys the poet's love through song; he has a vision of reunion after suffering (after being lost in "fatal tides" the "islands" will be found through the spiritual geography of the lover — "Blue latitudes and levels of your eyes") when the final mysteries ("secret oar and petals of all love") will be revealed.

The fifth section, however, presents a sad contrast. The lovers are now physically united once more, but the harmony is broken and love is dead. Waking past midnight, "lonely" though his lover is with him, the poet uses images of hardness, coldness, brittleness to suggest the broken relation. One image seems to be, proleptically, of a bridge with broken cables ("The cables of our sleep so swiftly filed, / Already hang, shred ends from remembered stars"). Moonlight is "deaf," tyrannous, inexorable as the tide, in contrast to the sympathetic moon of II. (The suggestion is also, of course, that this outcome is as inevitable as the tides.) The sky, instead of being mysteriously consanguine with the sea, is a "godless cleft . . . Where nothing turns but dead sands flashing" (the dead and meaningless moon). The lovers part, unable to communicate; as the sailor-lover leaves, the poet accepts the separation (even though he cannot understand it) and bids him farewell in a moving stanza.

The sixth and last section presents the poet's affirmation, in spite of everything, of his continued commitment to the sea (in all its meanings). Though he is "derelict and blinded," he continues to believe in the bond between sea and sky ("O rivers mingling toward the sky") and in the possibility of reaching the harbor which is as rare as the phoenix; though "thy waves rear / More savage than the death of kings" he still awaits "Some splintered garland for the seer." The second half of the poem describes the vision of reaching this harbor of resurrection and fulfillment. Belle Isle, "white echo of the oar" of love's mystery imagined at the end of IV, will contain the "lounged goddess" and will be found through the "imaged Word" (which will, presumably, correspond to "Creation's blithe and petalled word" once thundered to the "lounged goddess" of the island). It will transcend time, hold "Hushed willows anchored"; it will eliminate all betrayals and partings, making love perfect: "It is the unbetrayable reply / Whose accent no farewell can know." The amorous vision and the poetic vision, then, are one; the perfect Word (to which the perfect poem can be reduced) will also redeem love.

I have postponed discussion of "For the Marriage of Faustus and Helen," Crane's first long poem (written in 1922–23), because it seems best to consider it in relation to *The Bridge*, to which it is precursor and parallel. It is a very ambitious performance indeed, similar in intention to Joyce's *Ulysses* and Eliot's *Waste Land* in suggesting a fusion of present and past, a "bridge between so-called classic experience and . . . our seething, confused cosmos of today," in Crane's words. Of *The Waste Land*, Crane said, "After this perfection of death — nothing is possible in motion but a resurrection of some kind"; and this he hoped that his poem would provide. He described his plan thus in a letter: "Almost every symbol of current significance is matched by a correlative, suggested or actually stated, 'of ancient days.' Helen, the symbol of this abstract 'sense of beauty,' Faustus the symbol of myself, the poetic or imaginative man of all times. . . . Part II . . . begins with *catharsis,* the acceptance of tragedy through destruction . . . It is Dionysian in its attitude, the creator and the eternal destroyer dance arm in arm . . ." Actually, the Faustus-Helen symbolism is of very limited validity, not going far beyond the title (Crane seems not to have known Goethe's *Faust*; Marlowe was his only source), and the structural parallels between past and present are flimsy indeed. Though there are several fine passages, the poem seems to me of interest chiefly for the full embodiment of Crane's visionary theme in the last part: the fourth dimension, the mystical "lone eye," the Dionysian acceptance and transcendence of war, tragedy, and death. It was written not long after his mystical, or anesthetic, revelation in the dentist's chair and his commitment to the visionary poetic, with the Rimbaudian program of intoxication and derangement of the senses.

The Bridge was begun in 1923 as an attempt to carry further the kind of interpretation of modern life and its relation to the past that Crane had made in "For the Marriage of Faustus and Helen." The greater part of it was written during the visit to the Isle of Pines in 1926; but Crane was constantly occupied with the project, revising and adding to it, until its publication in 1930. Crane thought of it as his *magnum opus,* his poetic testament; he spoke of it as an epic like the *Aeneid,* planned like the Sistine Chapel, embodying the Myth of America, and refuting Eliot's pessimistic *Waste Land* to provide an affirmative interpretation of modern civilization. These rash and grandiose claims were demolished promptly and definitively by Allen Tate and Yvor Winters when the poem appeared. We may begin, therefore, by granting that *The Bridge* is not the Great American Epic, or any kind of epic, and that it is not a mature or responsible interpretation of American history or of the modern world. What kind of poem is it, then, and what kind of interest does it have now, after thirty-five years?

In his highly persuasive recent exegesis, Dembo calls it "a romantic lyric given epic implications" and defines its theme as "the exiled poet's quest for a logos in which the Absolute that he has known in his imagination will be made intelligible to the world. . . . . Crane tried to find in the history of American society some evidence that this society was capable of a psychological experience essentially identical with the poet's ecstatic apprehension of the Ideal as Beauty. The narrator in *The Bridge* thus journeys to a mythic Indian past that represents 'the childhood of the continent,' becomes an Indian himself, and marries Pocahontas in a ritual fire dance. Having thus learned the Word, attained the guerdon of the goddess, he returns to his own time . . . Although he now sees Pocahontas not as a fertile goddess, but as a sterile prostitute, the poet keeps his faith and concludes the poem with a hymn celebrating the Bridge as a modern embodiment of the Word."

The key Dembo finds in Nietzsche's theory of tragedy, which provided Crane "with a metaphysical argument with which to meet disillusion, whatever its source, and thus associated him not merely with Whitman, but with the whole tradition of optimism in nineteenth-century romantic literature:" "Simply put, Crane accepted the proposition that resurrection always follows suffering and death. That is really the essence of what he took from Nietzsche." Except for the emphasis on Nietzsche, and the consistency and penetration of supporting analysis, Dembo's thesis is not new; Yvor Winters long ago observed that Emerson and Whitman taught a similar doctrine, and he argued that Crane merely put it into practice, following it to its logical end of suicide. For most of us, Dembo's association of the doctrine with Nietzsche and the Dionysiac tradition makes it more palatable; but I cannot see that it answers any of the objections of Winters and Tate. We are, however, concerned primarily not with the intrinsic merits of the doctrine, but with its effectiveness as theme of the poem. Conceding it all possible efficacy as a unifying force, the unity of the poem remains very loose indeed, and some parts remain very much better than others.

The "Proem" begins with the image of the seagull in its poise and freedom (its "inviolate curve," as in Hopkins' "Windhover," which Crane had certainly not yet read, suggesting a balance of the forces of control and release). This image is contrasted with that of the file clerk in his confined routine work, taken aloft only by elevators, dreaming of sails, and with that of the denizens of the cinema who hope for revelation there. The Bridge is then evoked as a parallel to the seagull, uniting motion and stillness, freedom and necessity; though, ironically, the madman commits suicide by leaping from it. It is a symbol of the Divine, but its rewards are mysterious: its accolade is anonymity, but it also shows "vibrant reprieve and pardon." It is both harp and altar, threshold of the future, prayer of the outcast, and cry of the lover; it condenses eternity and cradles night. "Only in darkness is thy shadow clear" — and the poet, standing under it at night in winter and in the symbolic darkness of suffering, prays to it to take the place of his lost religious mythologies:

> Unto us lowliest sometime sweep, descend
> And of the curveship lend a myth to God.

The first section, "Ave Maria," is a monologue of Columbus as he is returning from his first voyage. Columbus is, of course, the poet-voyager, and Cathay is the terrestrial paradise, or the Absolute, or the Word. He praises God (and Crane notes that here the rhythm changes from the earlier "waterswell" to a suggestion of the "great *Te Deum* of the court, later held"), who "dost search / Cruelly with love thy parable of man" in experiences of which this voyage is a type, and testifies to awareness of His presence: "Elohim, still I hear thy sounding heel!"

The second section, "Powhatan's Daughter," has five subdivisions. The basic symbol is Pocahontas as the mythical body of

America to be explored and known, the past, the Absolute. "The Harbor Dawn" presents very beautifully the protagonist's vision of her, between sleeping and waking, in the modern city. In "Van Winkle" he merges with the legendary character from an older New York and takes the subway, which, in "The River," becomes the symbolically named "20th Century Limited" train; there is then the associated picture of the hobos, who with all their faults, "touch something like a key perhaps"; they remember the past and know the country: "They know a body under the wide rain." Both Tate and Winters consider "The River" the best part of *The Bridge*, with its description of the journey down the Mississippi as it appears both to the "Pullman breakfasters" on the modern train and to the hobos, who merge with the pioneers; there is no strained philosophy or symbolism, but a loving evocation of the country and the people, past and present, in concrete terms. "The Dance" follows, and is the climax of the section: the protagonist consummates his union with Pocahontas; he becomes Maquokeeta, an Indian, and is the sacrificial victim burned at the stake in a ritual death dance; he is then resurrected and symbolically united with Pocahontas, now become America. The poetry is intense and beautiful; but it is hard to forget Winters' comment: "one does not deal adequately with the subject of death and immortality by calling the soil Pocahontas, and by then writing a love poem to an imaginary maiden who bears the name of Pocahontas." With regard to the pantheism of the whole section, Winters remarked, "I believe that nothing save confusion can result from our mistaking the Mississippi Valley for God." The last part of the section, "Indiana," is a sentimental portrait of the pioneer woman; by common consent it is one of Crane's worst lapses.

"Cutty Sark," the third section, begins the loosely connected and generally less effective group that deal with the protagonist's effort to preserve his faith while living in a world that seems to deny the Ideal; it is this part that corresponds to Crane's description of the poem as an "epic of the modern consciousness." "Cutty Sark" Crane described as a fantasy on the period of the whalers and clipper ships, built on the plan of a fugue with two voices, one that of the pianola, expressing the Atlantis or Eternity theme, and the other that of the derelict sailor encountered in the South Street dive. On the way home, the protagonist sees a phantom regatta of clipper ships from Brooklyn Bridge; Crane uses the historical names, and meant the arrangement on the page to be significant: he called it a cartogram, and said "The 'ships' should meet and pass in line and type — as well as in wind and memory . . ." (In this section particularly, Crane's description of his intentions is more elaborate and more interesting than the achieved result.) Some commentators who have puzzled about the significance of the title seem not to have been aware that the trademark of "Cutty Sark" whisky is a clipper ship.

"Cape Hatteras" Crane described as a "kind of ode to Whitman." It is also an ironic celebration of the airplane as embodiment of the modern, its speed and its conquest of space. Man is drunk with power and blind with pride — "the eagle dominates our days" with its "wings imperious"; he neglects the past (the recurrent symbols of the eagle for space and the serpent for time here receive new emphasis) and the imaginative meaning of infinity. His technological triumphs have led only to more destructive war, and Crane evokes the dogfights of World War I. But the Falcon-Ace has "a Sanskrit charge / To conjugate infinity's dim marge" — in Dembo's interpretation, "to plumb beneath death to resurrection and thereby . . . define the Word." War is justified in that beyond it lies resurrection and a new understanding of the Word; Whitman gives him a rebirth of faith through his vision of the rebirth of the slain.

"Three Songs" portrays three distortions of love in the modern

37

world, perversions of the ideal Pocahontas. The most effective of them is "National Winter Garden," where the mythic dance is reduced to a burlesque show. "Quaker Hill" pictures the corruption of the countryside by commercialism and philistinism: the Quaker meeting house in Connecticut is now a weekend resort called the New Avalon Hotel.

"The Tunnel" describes, literally, the subway ride under the river to get to the bridge; figuratively, as the epigraph from Blake suggests, the final descent into the abyss before the ascent. Thus it is a kind of Inferno, a descent into hell, into the dark winter night before morning.

> The phonographs of hades in the brain
> Are tunnels that re-wind themselves, and love
> A burnt match skating in a urinal . . .

The protagonist sees himself in Poe, the martyred poet. But he emerges, "like Lazarus," to stand by the East River and look at the harbor he has been under.

"Atlantis," the final section, Crane called "A sweeping dithyramb in which the Bridge becomes the symbol of consciousness spanning time and space." It is ironic that this, the most ecstatic section of the poem, was the first to be completed. "Atlantis" presents the imagined fulfillment of the quest and the end of tragedy: "Vision of the Voyage," Cathay, Belle Isle, as seen by the archetypal voyager and quester Jason; the vision is "Deity's glittering Pledge," "Answerer of all," and the "white, pervasive Paradigm" of Love; it is, of course, the Bridge apotheosized. Perhaps it is ultimately the poetic imagination. The poet prays, "Atlantis, — hold thy floating singer late!" The image is a pathetic one, since the singer is floating because Atlantis is not there, and the poem ends on an unanswered question.

Tate seems to me to put his finger on the trouble with the symbolism of *The Bridge*. He observes that the framework of symbol in "For the Marriage of Faustus and Helen" "is an abstraction empty of any knowable experience." Crane became dissatisfied both with its style and with the "literary" character of the symbolism, and so "set about the greater task of writing *The Bridge*." But the Bridge "differs from the Helen and Faust symbols only in its unliterary origin. I think Crane was deceived by this difference, and by the fact that Brooklyn Bridge is 'modern' and a fine piece of 'mechanics.' . . . The single symbolic image, in which the whole poem centers, is at one moment the actual Brooklyn Bridge; at another, it is any bridge or 'connection'; at still another, it is a philosophical pun and becomes the basis of a series of analogies. . . . Because the idea is variously metaphor, symbol, and analogy, it tends to make the poem static. The poet takes it up, only to be forced to put it down again *when the poetic image of the moment is exhausted*. The idea does not, in short, fill the poet's mind; it is the starting point for a series of short flights, or inventions connected only in analogy — which explains the merely personal passages, which are obscure, and the lapses into sentimentality."

Crane had intended "For the Marriage of Faustus and Helen" to be an answer to the pessimism of the school of Eliot, and *The Bridge* was to be an even more complete answer. But, Tate comments, "There was a fundamental mistake in Crane's diagnosis of Eliot's problem. Eliot's 'pessimism' grows out of an awareness of the decay of the individual consciousness and its fixed relations to the world; but Crane thought that it was due to something like pure 'orneryness,' an unwillingness 'to share with us the breath released,' the breath being a new kind of freedom that he identified emotionally with the age of the machine." And, he observes, "I think he knew that the structure of *The Bridge* was finally incoherent, and for that reason . . . he could no longer believe even in his lyrical powers; he could not return to the early work and take it up where he had left off. Far from 'refuting' Eliot, his whole career is a vindication of Eliot's major premise — that the integrity of the individual consciousness has broken down."

Key West: An Island Sheaf is a small volume of twenty-two poems that Crane left ready for publication at his death. (It was not issued separately but forms one section of the *Complete Poems*.) Most of them were written during or soon after his stay on the Isle of Pines in 1926; Waldo Frank accompanied him, and they stayed on the plantation belonging to Crane's maternal grandmother until it was wrecked by a hurricane. Some of the poems, however, were plainly written later, the last being "The Broken Tower," begun in Mexico only two months before Crane's suicide. Aside from being presumably Crane's choice of the best poems he had produced during these years (apart from *The Bridge*), the poems are unified by tropical imagery and feeling, the juxtaposition of fecundity and waste, beauty and death. Most of them are lower keyed, more "representational," and therefore more accessible than the poems of *White Buildings*; they are also more objectively personal and more varied in themes and techniques. Most critics have regarded these poems as exhibiting a great falling-off from the earlier volume, perhaps largely because Crane himself took this view — and certainly a primary motive for his suicide was his belief that "The Broken Tower" testified to the failure of his powers. But Crane was emphatically wrong about this poem, and he may therefore have been wrong about the whole trend. At any rate, it is possible to judge these poems by standards other than Crane's own "visionary" one, and to avoid equating them too closely with his personal agony and disintegration. Looked at thus independently, the poems in *Key West* and many of those labeled "Uncollected Poems" in the *Complete Poems* show a resemblance to the recent trend sometimes called "poetry of experience" — the direct and open-textured poetry, similarly related to personal crises, of Robert Lowell's *Life Studies* and W. D. Snodgrass' *Heart's Needle*, for example.

The title poem, "Key West," is a kind of farewell to the U.S.A. and to the modern civilization of which it is the most advanced embodiment.

> Because these millions reap a dead conclusion
> Need I presume the same fruit of my bone
> As draws them towards a doubly mocked confusion
> Of apish nightmares into steel-strung stone?

The "apish nightmares into steel-strung stone" is a negative counterpart to the lines in "Recitative"; in that poem, skyscrapers could be redeemed, at least metaphorically, when "darkness, like an ape's face, falls away / And gradually white buildings answer day." But now the apish nightmares remain, and are embodied in the skyscrapers. The poet's only recourse is to go to his tropical island, while knowing that he cannot escape the modern world.

"O Carib Isle!" is about death in the tropics. Nothing mourns the dead: neither the "tarantula rattling at the lily's foot" nor the other creatures. Against the pitiless violence of the scene the poet can invoke only the fecundity of vegetation; but the wind — the most violent force of all, as in tropical hurricanes —"that knots itself in one great death — / Coils and withdraws. So syllables want breath." With no confidence in gainsaying death, the poet therefore asks where and what the ruler of this kind of nature is — the metaphor suggesting that He must be as bloodthirsty as the legendary Captain Kidd. The last three stanzas show the poet envisioning his own death in terms that are a kind of tropical equivalent of those of the Divine Comedy. He hopes that he can die under the "fiery blossoms" of the poinciana so that his "ghost" can ascend until "it meets the blue's comedian host." What he fears is a slow and helpless death like those of the "huge terrapin" overturned and spiked "Each daybreak on the wharf" to await slow evisceration; and, as he congeals, in the "satin and vacant" afternoons, he fears that the tropics are making him like the turtles. The shell (presumably both the shell of the poet as turtle and the island itself) is a gift of Satan; a "carbonic amulet" created by cosmic violence, "the sun exploded in the sea."

Only a few of the other poems in the volume can be mentioned. "The Idiot" is a vivid, uncomplicated, and very powerful rendering of an idiot boy whom Crane also describes in a letter: "When I saw him next he was talking to a blue little kite high in the afternoon. He is rendingly beautiful at times: I have encountered him in the road, talking again tout seul and examining pebbles and cinders and marble chips through the telescope of a twice-opened tomato can." The poem describes the embarrassment and ridicule he produces, with "squint lanterns in his head, and it's likely / Fumbling his sex . . ."; it presents the kite and tin-can telescope scene, and finally his song "Above all reason lifting"; the poet's "trespass vision shrinks to face his wrong." Quinn is probably right in suggesting that Crane sees the idiot implicitly as a distorted parallel to himself, a parody of the visionary poet, similarly derided and rejected. It is not necessary to read the poem in this way, but it helps to explain the moving quality it undoubtedly possesses. "Royal Palm" and "The Air Plant" — both in regular quatrains, like most of the poems in the volume — may be regarded as tropical "bridges," as Hazo suggests: the palm ascends to heaven and the air plant ("This tuft that thrives on saline nothingness") lives in air, welcoming hurricanes as well as breezes. Both poems are relatively simple, straightforward, and emblematic in technique; they are herbal equivalents of bestiaries like those of Marianne Moore, making the plants types of human qualities. "The Hurricane" evokes the power of an awesome divinity, its archaism suggesting the Old Testament god of the whirlwind. (There is an implicit parallel in several of these poems between the hurricane and the force of poetic inspiration.)

By common consent, the best poem in the volume, and one of Crane's greatest lyrics, is "The Broken Tower." Crane's letters give the background of the poem fully, and it is a very important and moving biographical document. Crane wrote it in February–March 1932, under the stimulus of his late and unexpected love affair with Peggy Baird. It was, of course, based on an actual experience of helping to ring the church bells at dawn in Taxco, Mexico. The poem testifies to his feeling of rebirth and integration both in what it says and in the fact of its existence, for it was the first poem Crane had been able to finish in two years. But the feeling of hope and confidence evaporated during the weeks of revision; the people to whom he sent the poem happened not to reply promptly; and Crane became convinced that the poem was a failure and that it proved his creative powers to be exhausted. This conviction was the basis of his despair in those fantastic final days in Mexico; with nowhere to go, feeling at a dead end, he alternated between drunken debauchery and paranoiac suspiciousness until the threats of suicide reached their inevitable conclusion. The poem can hardly be detached entirely from this biographical context — any more than can, say, the late sonnets of Keats or the "terrible sonnets" of Hopkins — or from the context of Crane's other poetry, and it derives added significance from the fact that it is a final triumphant affirmation of the visionary theme and a kind of poetic testament.

The basic image is the implicit identification of the utterance of the church bells and the utterance of the poet; both are expressions and embodiments of vision and of divine love. The poet himself is both the tower and the sexton within it, pulled up and down in exultation and despair as the sexton is by his work of pulling the bell ropes. (The images are inconsistent visually, but not thematically; the poet is in both cases the agent and vehicle of Poetry, which enslaves and destroys him.)

> The bells, I say, the bells break down their tower;
> And swing I know not where. Their tongues engrave
> Membrane through marrow, my long-scattered score
> Of broken intervals. . . . And I, their sexton slave!

The fifth stanza makes explicit the identification of the two kinds of music — or perhaps it would be better to say, the substitution of poetry for any other religion. The poet's dedication is religious: he has become a poet ("entered the broken world," become a broken tower) for no other purpose than to "trace the visionary company of love," however fleeting its voice. The next stanza, however, voices doubt of the validity of the identification. "My word I poured." But was it really divine, was it the Word? His blood supplies no answer; but "she / Whose sweet mortality stirs latent power" revives and reassures him so that he is "healed, original now, and pure . . . " Although the biographical reference is clear enough, in terms of the poem the "she" is also a psychic force, a feminine part of the personality (although there is no evidence that Crane ever read Jung, anyone who has can hardly avoid thinking of the Jungian *anima*) which brings about an integration of the personality (the new tower built within, not stone, for "Not stone can jacket heaven," but "slip of pebbles") and unites human and divine love. The tower in the last stanza becomes the brazen tower of Danaë which Zeus entered in a golden shower, thus uniting human and divine: "Unseals her earth, and lifts love in its shower." Whether this psychological resolution of the question of the status and origin of the vision seems satisfactory will depend on the reader's convictions; in terms of imagery and tonal climax, at least, it works brilliantly.

Many of Crane's poems raise the question of belief in a peculiarly urgent form. Not only do they proclaim allegiance to a "higher consciousness," a transcendent Vision attained through sexual passion or alcohol or art, but they exalt this dedication to ecstatic passion and death (with automatic resurrection) into a substitute religion, transferring to it the language and feeling of Christian devotion. This is particularly clear in the long poems, "For the Marriage of Faustus and Helen" and *The Bridge*. One's final judgment in this matter cannot be separated from one's religious and aesthetic beliefs. A number of able critics have recently asserted the claims of Neo-Romanticism in its various forms — Dionysiac ecstasy, vision, occultism, and mysticism — as against Eliotian classicism. My own view is that the formulations of Tate and Winters are still accurate: Crane was the "archetype of the modern American poet whose fundamental mistake lay in thinking that an irrational surrender of the intellect to the will would be the basis of a new morality" (Tate); "a poet of great genius, who ruined his life and his talent by living and writing as the two greatest religious teachers of our nation recommended" (Winters). Whether Crane took the doctrine primarily from Whitman and Emerson, as Winters thought, or from Nietzsche, as Dembo argues, makes no fundamental difference, nor does Quinn's attempt to make it respectable by associating it with Maritain's "creative intuition." Dembo's emphasis on the primacy of aesthetic reference in the doctrine — the poet seeking the absolute — makes it less repugnant; but it was more than aesthetic, it was the only religion Crane had. If we take it seriously as such, it is hard to see how it can be called (to use Eliot's criteria) a mature or coherent or responsible interpretation of the meaning of life and death. Aside from the odor of spilt religion, there is a feeling of strain in those poems in which the doctrine is presented explicitly, rather than as embodied in specific experience. This feeling, together with the ultimate incommunicability and obscurity of the doctrine in itself, is, I think, responsible for many of Crane's failures. Sometimes his linguistic effects — such as "adagios of islands" — seem not to correspond to any experience of poet or reader; they can be explained (as Crane brilliantly explained this one), but they still appear contrived and therefore ultimately mere tricks. Similarly, the symbolic structure of Crane's two long poems is abstract and "willed," standing for no real experience. Crane's "doctrine," then, is both shoddier and more dangerous than Yeats's "system"; and immensely less viable in poetry. Yeats's system enabled him to "hold reality and justice in a single thought"; Crane's allowed him too often to transcend, or to ignore, both.

Crane had no messianic ambitions, however, and it is unfair to him to overstress the "doctrine." In general, he seems to me most completely successful when he has a subject other than the pure visionary gospel, one that takes him outside himself and provides a dramatic situation. I have indicated by my choice of poems to discuss which I think are his best. After all possible reservations and subtractions have been made, there remain a substantial number of great lyrics, unique, splendid, and powerful; and these are enough. In the other poems — the minor successes and partial failures — there are unforgettable passages, images, phrases. Crane exploits the resources of the verbal medium to and sometimes beyond its limits; his language is always charged with meaning (to recall Pound's definition of poetry) and it never lacks excitement and challenge. At his best, he has a directness and immediacy, a haunting intensity and candor that are unlike anything else in English poetry.

✒Selected Bibliography

Works of Hart Crane

White Buildings: Poems by Hart Crane. Foreword by Allen Tate. New York: Boni and Liveright, 1926.

The Bridge. Paris: Black Sun Press; New York: Liveright, 1930.

The Collected Poems of Hart Crane, edited with an Introduction by Waldo Frank. New York: Liveright, 1933. (Includes the essay "Modern Poetry.")

The Letters of Hart Crane, 1916–1932, edited by Brom Weber. New York: Hermitage House, 1952.

Current American Reprint

The Complete Poems of Hart Crane, edited with a Foreword by Waldo Frank. Garden City, N.Y.: Anchor (Doubleday). $.95.

Bibliography

Rowe, H. D. *Hart Crane: A Bibliography.* Denver: Swallow, 1955.

Biographies

Horton, Philip. *Hart Crane: The Life of an American Poet.* New York: Norton, 1937. (Includes as appendixes an essay and several letters by Crane explaining his beliefs about poetry in general and his specific intentions in some of his own poems.)

Weber, Brom. *Hart Crane: A Biographical and Critical Study.* New York: Bodley Press, 1948. (Includes previously uncollected poetry and prose.)

Critical Studies

Dembo, L. S. *Hart Crane's Sanskrit Charge: A Study of* The Bridge. Ithaca, N.Y.: Cornell University Press, 1960.

Hazo, Samuel. *Hart Crane: An Introduction and Interpretation.* New York: Barnes and Noble, 1963.

Quinn, Vincent. *Hart Crane.* New York: Twayne, 1963.

MONROE K. SPEARS

Articles and Parts of Books

Alvarez, Alfred. *Stewards of Excellence: Studies in Modern English and American Poets.* New York: Scribner's, 1958. Pp. 107–23.

Blackmur, R. P. *Form and Value in Modern Poetry.* Garden City, N.Y.: Doubleday Anchor Books, 1957. Pp. 269–85.

Cambon, Glauco. *The Inclusive Flame. Studies in American Poetry.* Bloomington: Indiana University Press, 1963. Pp. 120–82.

Dembo, L. S. "Hart Crane's Early Poetry," *University of Kansas City Review,* 27:181–87 (1961).

Frank, Waldo. *In the American Jungle.* New York: Farrar and Rinehart, 1937. Pp. 96–108.

Friar, Kimon, and J. M. Brinnin, editors. *Modern Poetry: American and British.* New York: Appleton-Century-Crofts, 1951. Pp. 449–56.

Friedman, Paul. "*The Bridge*: A Study in Symbolism," *Psychoanalytic Quarterly,* 21:49–80 (1952).

Gregory, Horace, and Marya Zaturenska. *A History of American Poetry: 1900–1940.* New York: Harcourt, Brace, 1946. Pp. 468–81.

Koretz, Gene. "Crane's 'Passage,'" *Explicator,* vol. 13, no. 8, item 47 (1955).

Matthiessen, F. O. "American Poetry, 1920–1940," *Sewanee Review,* 55:24–55 (1947).

Miller, James E., Jr., Karl Shapiro, and Bernice Slote. *Start with the Sun: Studies in Cosmic Poetry.* Lincoln: University of Nebraska Press, 1960. Pp. 137–65.

Rosenthal, M. L. *The Modern Poets: A Critical Introduction.* New York: Oxford University Press, 1960. Pp. 168–82.

Tate, Allen. *Collected Essays.* Denver: Swallow, 1959. Pp. 225–37, 528–32.

Waggoner, Hyatt Howe. *The Heel of Elohim: Science and Values in Modern American Poetry.* Norman: University of Oklahoma Press, 1950. Pp. 155–92.

Winters, Yvor. *In Defense of Reason.* New York: Swallow and Morrow, 1947. Pp. 575–603. (Same essay in *On Modern Poets.* New York: Meridian Books, 1959. Pp. 120–43.)

48